Inside the Heart

A Book of Poetry

By

Ryan Fredric Steinbeck

Acknowledgements and Thank You:

Thanks to my wife, Cindy, for the love and inspiration to continue my journey.

Thanks to my family and friends who have supported me.

Also thanks to the poets, musical artists, and writers who continue to provide inspiration.

TABLE OF CONTENTS:

TO THE READER:

The writing of this book began over two years ago during my last book, *One House Left Standing*. It was the longest process of any project to date. I think it's because much of the dust in my life has settled and I'm looking at the world with a much calmer mind and heart. It was the most difficult because it's more about my journey than ever before. I felt, for the first time, I wrote without demons flying out of the box.

The name of this collection was decided upon before I began writing it, which is unusual for me. I typically need a flagship poem before I can decide on a title. *Inside The Heart* started out as an untitled, fragmented idea that I was unhappy with. It wasn't until a year later that it grew into what it is today. It was then that I realized where I was going with this, even though I must've known it all along because many poems written before have similar themes.

One poem stands out to me in particular. *Eternity* was written after I met a man who loved his wife dearly, and believed that vacationing with her provided essential growth in their relationship. He purchased an eight day Nepal/Kathmandu package where they rode elephants on a pilgrimage to neighboring towns, and slept under the stars in stilt houses. The moral of his story was that he and his wife had already purchased tombstones, which he described as an angel resting on a heart shaped carving which joins the two stones. He said he wanted to be by his wife's side for eternity. I can relate but I don't feel I said it as eloquently as he did.

Many of my poems go through several edits before I'm happy with them. But this collection was raw in that many ideas weren't altered much from their original state, even though I tried. Over all, the process was trying and difficult, but therapeutic and fun. I hope you get as much out of it as I've put into it.

Thank you for opening this book.

Ryan Steinbeck

Inside The Heart

Stolen from an alter ego
A shadowed shattered shell of myself
The foundation cracked
The safety net broken
A life once suspended now disentangled
A pilgrimage of faith and time
A voice from another side

Bound by secrets among obscurities
A sheltered demise disguised as optimism
Hands held in prayer for hope to arrive
A vanishing act among friends and principle
A cursed shadow between minions
Outside of biased acceptance
That formerly embraced who I was

The dawn on the horizon calls out
To till fields uncultivated
To sow seeds unplanted
To discover the last uncharted course
To the solitary arrival of significance
It all comes down to love and absolution
For the rite of passage inside the heart

All My Life

I make no apology
I want to be in your spirit
To serve the core of you
To triumph over eternity

Your vision draws me into black
In a whirlwind of mystification
A collision of expectation and certainty
Leaves the fiber of conclusion threadbare

Your discovery at world's end
In the darkest depths of imagery
If you were my alternate reality
I would break through to the other side

You're a foretelling of my end game
The difference between what's said and what's true
One million soul searches end the same
All my life I've been looking for you

She Is

An ocean dispersing my particles
Then recreating them
In an atmosphere of clouds

A higher place
A plateau not all can reach
The wind that answers my call

A telegraph of hope
A reflection of significance
Like a beautiful message of truth

A sunset after a storm
An age of new philosophy
A journey with no ending

Only Way

Innocence at its measure
Thoughts rise from the East
Mutation of perspective
Incredulity weighs persuasive
Chasing tails of fringe acceptance
Measures close at hand

Limitations facing reality
Grasping wings of awareness
Falling into ancient dreams
With contemporary demise
We come back to the start
With lessons in mind
Weapons in hand

A sun rise in hours
Belief is sought
Before becoming myth
Before time is misplaced

I share myself unlike before
As if it is Christmas day
I am here with you now
This is what called for destiny
This is my only way

Poles

Handcuffed to the sky
With feet in quagmire
The poles between us
Are of opposite forces

My wires undercast
I dig beneath for a current
My memory deleted in transition
By a method of rediscovery

My true magnetic north
Gives way to zero declination
The sum of my existence
Has become my navigation

A bridge of ice before me
Rivers of degradation behind
Secular minds commuted
In a feast of deliverance

Internal forces grow thermal
Detection on the periphery
The core melds loose elements
We become antipodal

Glimpse

We watched the grass grow
On the sun painted ground
Shadows resume their spaces
Through the trees an opening

We catch a glimpse of the horizon
The next story it will tell
We knew it was inevitable
Still sooner than we thought

With the clear turned to glossy
Reason follows to mystery
Realism holds disastrous insensitivity
As we try to quantify this history

A stake in the final hours
Is my closing requisition
To be there as you were for me
When it's time to rest your head

Now

Twilight enters
The tread of day broken
My mind's in regress
We lay down our heads

Banter of self-importance
The systematic annoyances of life
I'm not ready to move on
You know and you linger

If I could give you the planets as tokens
I'd find a way to breathe in outer space
I'd stop all time before us
All I want right here is now

My Composition

Some time has passed
Since the testimony of your soul
The looking glass into your heart

No immunization of consciousness
Wounds are not healed
A missionary spreading the word
About loss without death

Unseasonably high clouds
Give way to open skies
No armor to put a chink into

Confusing window signs
A daylight disguise for nighttime warfare
A sudden change in air pressure
After hints of rebellion

Exiled to the southern fragment of the universe
For setting fire to the family tree
I can't be free with a collar around my neck
It's just my composition

On My Own Two Feet

On my own two feet
I am no longer deceived
By change of direction
By the course of secrets

I see my sails above
I see the horizon expanded
I set fire to a new sky
In a sea of isolation

The haunted depths of tribulation
I discover my heart's symbol
I discredit previous liturgy
As I open up the atmosphere

I denounce accepted dialogues
I am no longer divided
In the sea I will not be swallowed
This will not be my grave

Standing in a pocket of light
I avoid the mossy growth
The waves attack the floorboards
On my own to feet I remain

Wave And Whisper

Finding God on the floor in a dark room
Of a run down hotel
In the remains of a nightmare

On the stage with truth and fiction disheveled
There's no more sentiment
For loss of light

Danger and disaster are acquaintances
Drawing in under the façade of temptation
Recognizing weakness prior to attack

A wave and a whisper
Sends a helix of shudders
Down perfidious spines

Desire fashioned by their treaties
Searching for something they don't need
Discovering something they don't want

Trip Wire

Breathing is like talking to ghosts
As you challenge the sun in the sky
Wings spread across the shoreline
Another no show when it mattered most

A shift in procession
With edges unchanged
Truth inhales in the middle
Of distorted optimism

Strangled in a house on fire
A harvesting of poisons
Oblivious to the trip wire
Determined to validate your point

Sanctity from sheltered eyes
Whimsical on the surface of ruin
It's time to divest the fear depriving you
It's time to embrace the certainty

Code Of Silence

A head of armor
Marching into the unknown
When your senses weaken
Your search begins

Under a code of silence
Open pretense
Ready for self-defense
As you watch the sky fall

Flowers in disguise
Building a second chance
Loosen your grip
Your bag of tricks left behind
Ready to give this way a try

No more word search
Surrender to the course ahead
With the ground under foot
Your tremors diminish

A soul once extorted
Found in the separation
From the words of violence
In a code of silence you remain

Same Good Thing

Calling to mind is arduous
When my quest is diligence
When my wheels are spinning
While standing in place
I am in another world
With senses rattled
I don't mean any harm
The waters of notion are murky
Everyday I endeavor your honor
Awed that I weaken

Moments like years without you
Hesitation owns my reactions
Everyday with you feels novel
I want to be better for you
With intentions documented
I locate my location
You're the thoughts in my mind
The beating of my heart
You are my center and circumference

When there's nothing to propose
When I continue to dig this hole
When I make the worst of circumstance
When I contradict my thoughts
When I think there's nothing left
You're the good thing about me

Building up from the ground
Through the pain you've been through
I hope there comes a day
When I'm the same good thing about you

Sense Of Worth

It's difficult to put a finger on
The pulse of predictability
A limitless supply of excuses
Voices from misdirected shadows
No space between wisdom or behavior
As you measure your sense of worth

I used to enjoy standing
On the outskirts of fundamental principle
No commitment to truths that might restrain me
No one wants a stubborn, cold heart.

In the end there's a need to feel
That should've been there from the start
With the finish line in sight
I'm recognizing a sense of worth

Accomplishments dissolved instantaneously
By the jealousy of her heart
By the need to be the center
Of the shipwreck that became us

It could've been avoided
With reassurance beyond words
With acknowledgement of generations past
With time spent on more than your feelings
With planning how to raise a child
With letting go

The definition of a circle
The apprentice becomes the teacher
The lesson taught should be learned
The mirror shows your reflection
But you still need to look

Stepping outside yourself
You'd see a world of volatility
Adults who are still children
Children who want to grow

When you reflect upon your life
Measuring your success
Will it be how much you have
Or how much you've lost?

There were road blocks and impasses
That may have been avoided
There were times to be the savior
Instead of demanding one yourself

There were days when a simple smile
Would've suggested a world of selflessness
Instead the door closed
Never to reopen

If you wonder what happened
If you're looking to allocate blame
Had you simply taken the time
To infuse a sense of worth
It might not be this way

Staging

Many years have passed
A modern winter staging
The same time of day draws near
I participate in buoyant delusion

Yearning for unchanged dislocation
Burrowing in reminiscence
The magnificence of our sadness
Obscured by transience

Unavoidable disambiguation
Of postulation misinterpreted
Rivers stepped in once too many
As objectives in disguise

Elevation of conjecture underneath
I watched your eyes turn downward
The moment before I stumbled
In the commencement of first light

Ice

Ice forms on the engines
As we prepare to launch
The crystal sky condemning
Demeanor of potent aspiration

We try to live in ice houses
Persistently setting fires
A culmination of insoluble history
We deny predestined thoughts

To melt my frozen heart
Even though I can't melt yours
Is to know the idea of freedom
Is greater than authenticity

From the icy bank above
I watch the river's resolve
It has a destination
Always it flows to the ocean

Duration of life
In the coldest of winters
A pulse still strong
In a war of seasons

Persistence begs for renewal
A homecoming of descending foliage
The ice formed between us
Thaws in the equinox sun

Two Sides

When there is more discretion
Until the disease fits the medication
We are friends and strangers
In defense of terrain

Broadcasting innocence
Duplicity behind the scenes
The two sides to this story
Both turn a deaf ear

Empathy and compromise
Foreign words of native tongue
In a land of neutral distinction
We hide association

Views exchanged for negation
In a setting claimed for tranquility
Propagation of cooperation
As they turn the other cheek

Maybe dig a little deeper
Maybe look in a mirror
Maybe try a different angle
We're supposed to be united after all

Hands Up

We build to an end
With no end in sight
A message loud and clear
Never received

I can't see the horizon anymore
Where it begins or ends
I'm the distance in your mind
Thousands of miles departed

With my hands up
I walk forward in surrender
I'm encircled in disclaimer
Neither of us will let go

You're a ticking time bomb
Dynamite with a short fuse
The heart of coldest winters
A countdown to extermination

A lovesick drifter
I've walked a half-life in circles
Waiting for the other shoe to drop
Before I fade away

My hands reach higher than before
Fingers barely touch the ledge
I climb the rungs to new ground
Somehow you were still waiting

Leaves From Heaven

A quiet conversation
In a silent forgiving land
A gentle breeze the private spectator

Early spring as the prospect
Buds forming on distant trees
Set in motion our surprise

Crackle on the roof top
Then the street behind
Then right before our feet

We turn our gaze aloft
Miles into the clear sky
Dead leaves falling from heaven

Now I'm looking up again
Anything has become possible
As a moment to remember

The Mystery That Will Always Be

Eyes like statutes
Her pillars on the ocean side
Remains of a civilization
That's lost its fight with time

She is a tangible illusion
The mystery that will always be
A sun in an dreary sky
Experienced in burning skin

She pulls the earth from both sides
It unravels like yarn
How she came to change the tide
A mystery that will always be

Once fearful of the sun
I now bathe in the sea
In a cloudless sky
The mystery that will always be

Always Been

Looking out and forward
No time to make time
Accrual of wrong turns
Actions louder than words

Bidding on the highest excuse
Holding the cards
Pointing fingers
Passing out blame

Light at the end of the tunnel
Train of realism
Feeling the radiance
Deciding on direction

Catalogues of insults
Keep the sky grounded
Assigning victims
Out of misinterpretation

A third incarnation
Adjusting the laws again
I'm still waiting, hoping
You know I've always been

Pitch Black

A deafening silence fills my head
Unsure if my eyes are open
I can't feel past the wall of fear
The cold ground of emptiness

Lying face up
I remember losing my footing
The scent of musty soil around me
An anthology of unintelligible thought

Stillness broken for an instant
Movement in the surroundings
Maybe an angel's wings
As I withdraw from suspension

I interpret survival's whisper
Forcing me to stand
My eyes grow accustomed
To the varying shades of black

Arms out ahead
I reach a spot of light
A window in the earth above
When memory shakes from hibernation

Climbing the cold wet rocks
Nervous energy makes hours from minutes
Inner eternity cloaks me in sunlight
As I reach into the blue sky above

Above The Clouds

There are always consequences
Last miles are walked alone
Feeling the untried incline
Competing with thinning air

Internal antagonism lessens
A coherent voice of reason
Unawareness no longer in command
Above the clouds

Sanctuary in your presence
Every day another reason
Why you run through these veins
And inside the heart

New heights on this cold day
With vastness recalculated
No avenues disregarded
In the act of signification

Long term visibility
We befriend the sun in vacant skies
With my feet still set on earth
Above the clouds

International Waters

I believed rumors of a starry night
Looking up I saw canopy
If this wasn't reality
You would never let me know

I was unable to row the boat
At the bottom of the ocean
An entire world out there
Through a door you wouldn't open

We scattered like ashes in the wind
You blame the blaze ignited by your match
There are no actions to defend
You can't make water out of land

You still preach the prophecy
Even now they believe you
I've seceded to international waters
Disbelieving the reform is true

On this day I recognized
The canopy could be removed
The daylight now brighter
The stars look down nightly

There are millions of lies on the horizon
All could be disproved
My new freedom from ancient times
Bares the futility of this fight

State Of Mind

A matriculate in a dying system
A stranger in a strange land
Accused of muliebrity in a man's world
The past escapes in hindsight

Regions, borders, and titles abound
Subsequent the tactless course
Fearing the inside is out
After death of true importance

Hollow affiliations
Substitutes for ideology
Perception is not always reality
It's all a state of mind

A dance of dissolution
The state of affairs marches on
One eye blind and the other closed
As a choice to be unkind

A flood of acceptance begins under skin
Throw your hand or let it play out
There's still time to starve the anger
It's all a state of mind

Reflection

She's scared of looking in the mirror
What could be looking back
She can see the distance clearer
Than she can see herself

Never does she wonder
There's not a day she doesn't cry
In the reflection before her
Is the past she left behind

Bravery lifts her eyes
As her image plays tricks
A troubled soul exposed
Surrounded in her history

The axis of perception turns
With a simple change of heart
Take some time for self-reflection
To change your point of view

Bridge To Burn

I grew up in a barren land
Desolance the only companion
I kept my head enduringly turned
To ignore the dogs in the manger

There was a town over the distant hill
A different way of life
Until a shadow cast and it went dark
They told me it was such a traitorous place

I retained that vision in mind
My curiosity invaded
Evidence of good deeds reached us one day
But they allege it was misconstrued

Under my hat I kept hope
Until darkness pilfered it from my mind
I became accustomed with going to the well
Instead of going the extra mile

Eventually I went my own way
With the thought that I'd return
To play both ends against the middle
There was still a bridge to burn

Burn it did when the lies ousted truth
From a poison seed planted long ago
I called to mind that town again
Just as in decades past

It took years to erase the bias
To build up the audacity
To finally walk inside the radius
My arrival a homecoming

Favorite Prince

They cheer their favorite prince
He smiles and waves to the serfs
Behaving just as they'd asked
Hiding a vandalized soul

His eyes in the midst of straying
He dreams about the river
Where he saw his reflection
To obey the forces of reckoning

They gave him castles of gold
He only longed for mountains
He dreams about the day
To leave the bait of falsehood

They worship his image
They give what they would want
He should give them what they need
His true identity ignored

The irony of this prince
A master as servant
A rebellion at hand
He abandons the kingdom

With a heart under siege
No wind in his bearing
An explanation measured as betrayal
Kin erase their memory

Love ties loose ends
He takes the reigns of Romeo
Constantly falling short
Never trained to ride the horse

His princess demonized
Not of royal blood
He ineradicably flees his domain
Refusing these sacrifices
Nor to sleep with ignorance
Nor live life pretending
Nor be self-sacrificial
Nor carry the guilt of his empire

They watch the drawbridge close
With fear and freedom in his eyes
He takes her hand and lifts her up
They ride to destination unknown

Prince and princess on the run
But they have each other
Now it's everything they need
Never to be seen again

The Things I Wish I Could Say

The transmission source was lost
Truth doesn't come around here anymore
Interchanging parts with comparable results
Eradication is subtle

Decide what flag you believe
Decide what story you'll read
Even winning takes its toll
When there is no true end

I'm a mark of calamity
My train nearing derailment
Keep a lookout crossing the tracks
For the new innovation of silence

A holiday from suspension of disbelief
A unexpected ravine
The nightmares are your sacrifice
The morning delivers emptiness

The circularity of your contemplation
The pecking order in your head
The things I wish I could say
Are better left unsaid

Identity Of A Broken Man

In the mirror a man worth saving
From a history of revision
You forget your last memory
The identity of a broken man

A runaway train on the street
You lose your way back
Life is a sequence of midnights
As you faithlessly seek meaning

Amidst the tyranny of proclaimed saints
You see the fear in their eyes
You feel betrayal in their touch
As they condemn you for your crimes

Weapons fired in reluctance
Daggers thrown in defense
At the core is a plea for peace
Lost in unawareness

It won't end in the fire of forgiveness
You characterize fear and shame
Internalize anger and lamentation
The identity of a broken man

It can't go on forever
Only one hundred years or more
Your appeal is that of persuasion
In the face of absolute judgment

Every day you return home
You barter with common sense
Hoping to explain the story
Behind the identity of a broken man

When The World Watches

To wear hope as the emblem of life
Is to be human before affiliation
Before thought
Before policy

When one has strength
Lifting the other up
Setting back on course
When called upon

Not only when the world watches
Or we will crumble
Keep an open heart
Count blessings in sunrise

In the dead of winter
One leaf remains on this tree
Through the strongest wind it endures
Persistence of life is eternal

Fathom

Three days until arrival
The ceremony of flags circle the world
Starboard on a starry night
Among a gathering of many he knows no one

They are all hopeful lovers
As they sail across the ocean
All fears left on the dock
Resistance left in the shallows

Silence and time
The journey becomes the destination
Conscience of spirit in body
As he lies entangled with fate

For him it's about connection
About relinquishing control
The space between thoughts and words
Drown fathoms beneath him

The sky has an open heart
He flows through the veins
The immortality of the moment
Is all he'd hoped it would be

Elizabethtown

She is a blasting zone
Inside my mind's decanter
Falling rocks of theory
Cover the bones of my being

Violence of noise
In nighttime cylinders
Cliffs of emergence
From a higher plateau

It was lonely up there
I was insistently reaching
Until then I hadn't realized
How far Elizabethtown was from Eden

Decadent entourage
Decorated soul
I confused ordinary and perfect
When follower posed as leader

Escapists lost their touch
We waited for the barricade
Before we merged
Still, we merged

In a box full of mystery
Where I'm fated to reside
Inside the heart of life
With a welcoming committee

Piercing light negative
Image reveals an elusive truth
A designer's flaw kept me climbing
When I should've been coming down

Providence

Constant intention of position
The latest variety of fairy-tales
Physical and spiritual advent in equal tense

I explore the air streams
This might not give me up
New refuge in elevated sense

An overture of consternation
Running from the irreversible
No assertion of alternatives
Before the last night of reflection

Careful contemplation
A tutorial to conclude this conclusion
As I'm unable to unearth a defense
Now begins the resurgence
Welcome to providence

Passage

I had to call you out
A system of checks and unbalance
In a year of integration

You were the better pretender
Endeavoring to dismantle and deny
The mechanism you created

The same blood flowing in our rivers
Will now be divided
By our process of filtration

A shadow over a promised land
We will forever be tied and traced here
Where we are prisoners among common folk

With my wrists raw and bruised
I find passage to worlds unexplored
Where there are true laws of man

I am released among the masses
I see freedom on their faces
I see songs in their eyes

Their smiles welcoming
I sense a feeling of home
Wrapped in absence of falsehood

My origin woven in new science
The best facets are refined
My settlement is now permanent

Mission

Cold light on the riverbed
A prayer for snow
During a silent assault of raindrops

Good and evil
Always fate
Nothing unequivocal

Love won't keep us alive
There are no corners
No rules as a guide

Truth lives within
The route of location
Leads to the heart

A setting sun sparks nightfall
The day will be revisited
When nothing lasts forever

When the life of the mission
Comes to terms with fate
The greatness of daylight is observed

Executioner

Footprints in the mind
Waves of dissimilarities
Excavation of rebuttal
With a stranger in the house

The common flight of sin
A replication in the mirror
Of blood now thickening
In a pool of ascension

No longer open for discussion
Your attack of silence is trivial
Reaction is a malevolent inspiration
After static of misinterpretation

Curious eyes observe
The magician's sleight of hand
Once an asset among the elite
Now an object of aggression

Believing you hold the course of wisdom
The ability to pass judgment
On the day of accusation
When you're the executioner

All The Love In The World

Your cavalry returns home
Injured promises in tact
Spreading broken knowledge
It's better to steal than to give

You polish your craft in real time
A master of disguise
Crying alone at the end of ways
No one leaves the light on for you

A collection of souls in a jar
Remains on a dust gathered shelf
All the love in the world before you
Ravaged by the origin of duplicity

We are two sides of the same coin
Different sights are set
A declaration time and again
You were love's dark side on display
When all the love in the world
Didn't matter to you anyway

Can't Control The Rain

I see you've scattered rain
All over your town
I can see the bottom
Of my whisky bottle

I see the dark side of your face
Visible only in shadows
I watch you take shelter
From the storm you summoned

It's the storm that created you
With more darkness than can be spoken
What you've given
Has been left in the open

The chill in your bones
Will merge with your soul
Gambling with your sympathy
Will win you nothing

Someday your analogy
Will outgrow your blueprint
The shrine of your philosophy
Will expose your truth

Until then you're tinted
With a shade of gray
Let history books bring justice
To a crime ignored
When the town of believers
See you at first light
I'll be a million miles disappeared
Teaching the contrary of your apprenticeship
I don't expect to see you again
But I can't control the rain

Rode The Wave

An aberration not a mistake
We rode the wave
Eventually coming to shore

I remember you like childhood
Forever was a long time ago
When there's nothing to return to

I hope there is memory
That brings about a fondness
About years passed

I know that you know
Our real story didn't begin
Until our chapter came to an end

Piece

My ending was her beginning
From a past divided
That never parted

I thought my pieces where a whole part
Only a desolate road
With no stars above

A chink in my armor
She wedged inside like a swarm of bees
Then looked into my darkness

Now this forsaken course has an ending
Now there is a destination
Now new stars form constellations

My eyes are adjusting
As a soft light is rising
From a path only just revealed

Time is a consolation
Setting everything into place
She is my missing piece

Palms

Trampled ground
Eager for sun
Blind leading blind
Imploring for sight

Stillness settles between my palms
As an old friend in the night
This last deliberation
Masquerading as remedy

Without warning
Without condition
Turning corners
Then disappearing

My voice a distress signal
Reverberation of ancient times
I've turned some corners too
If you ever have any doubts

Weapons Of Mass Distraction

Hands digging in the dirt
A level playing field so you've heard
She is taking me at my word
As my operation remains covert
She's only guilty of one minor infraction
Weapons of mass distraction

Solitude plays a guessing game
Leaving doubt with the intent
You know she's heaven sent
And you are just lame
One day you'll understand the rules of attraction
Weapons of mass distraction

A round table discussion
With merchants in the arena
Vultures circle overhead
You look to control your inevitable eruption
All of this to initiate a reaction
Hot headed as the night draws to a close
By now you're hoping that she knows
But the idiot across the room wins the prize
You never succeed if you never try
I can't get no satisfaction
Weapons of mass distraction

Direction

The North Star my orientation
My life's anonymity
My soul's mirror
My reflection

Ever growing is my belief
In a postulated vision
With an open heart
The truth is spoken

A premeditated prospect
Eternally mutable
If we believe in our integration
Then my direction is undeniable

Last Hint Of Summer

She was the last hint of summer
The last dream of waves crashing the beach
Now a cold front approaches from the north

Vacationers leave for home
The town lay in a quiet slumber
I look to this land
With a stirring under my exterior

The last to make sense
Never within reach
Just a warm night in winter

To feel cold again
To miss the tempo of her life
To hope for summer again
So she'll remember my name

Omission of the third act
Reciting the lines of an old play
They know the missing scene
Everyone dreams about the last hint of summer

Eye

The periphery was ground zero
A crusade to destroy materialistic
Seven seconds changed perspectives
At mercy of a power uncontainable

Looking to the universe above
Inside a quarter mile of calm
With the eye as the center
Surrounded by chaos

An alter of blessings counted
In the heart of sanity
Fragments of his life
Flash before his eyes
And rotate around his head

Morning Sun

Red with eyes closed
Distant uprising
Feasting on the horizon
Weaving a new beginning

Welcome the morning sun
It stops the bleeding
Warming frozen hearts
Constructing its proposal

I'm not original sin
For speaking my mind
For living my life
For refusing to lie

Catch as light the origin of day
Mobilize the illumination armies
Aggressive elation of life draws near
As the first ray over tree tops

Bitter view turns bright
Magnetic sky an ornament
Morning sun an addiction
Waiting for the moment

Moonlight

I could tiptoe across the stars
True love in zero gravity
Oceans of solar wind
Caress the space around me

I could forget and forgive
The internal damage to my heart
As I left the atmosphere
Believing I'd land in safety
On my way down

Suspension and perpetuation
Worlds of dignity discovered
The right choice this time
As I'm cleared to land

A silhouette in moonlight
Pressure is stabilizing
Being present is truth
Tossing and turning at night
Waking to a new setting
Your spirit is my arrival

Perception

For years I ran in circles
Wearing a path in my head
A drifter of consciousness
In a charade of imagination

The scenery from my window
Took on a different angle
Still familiarity
Though a distant memory in my heart

My travel to the peak
Too remote to turn around
New followers cheer below
Encouragement is strength
Disbelievers move aside
They prefer the one who didn't climb

Suspended in their cage
As they encouraged me to live free
Too young to know the difference
To see the contradiction

A closed door of perception
A sign posted on the handle
The boy who once hid here
Has now found his way home

Eternity

If there's an age gap in heaven
Then the fire in the sky
Will carry us to answers
Then lead us home

A lot to be said of leaving
More about moving on
The sub plots are tied up
Only the main story remains

The stone is carved
Where an angel rests its head
The shape of a heart is a message
We are one for eternity

Ashore

I don't have a label
No fine print or disclaimer
Years of excavation
Revealed my heart

I only ever had a blind side
I could only ever see my side
The demons of my past were set free
After years on standby

Retracing steps with new shoes
Rediscovering long forgotten intimations
Partition from miscalculation
Now it's time to move on

Rocks and canyons of disenchant
Misappropriated as knowledge
Belief isn't always awareness
Faith isn't always blind

The future orbits around me
I see your land ahead
With rite of passage granted
My search ends as I come ashore

Goodbye

The day is masked by rolling smog
We as tenants rent land, water
A microcosm of a world at large
Awakens evils with each stone turned

Contaminated insight of reality
A dominion already claimed
Billions of years at peace
Stare down the loss of balance and reason

No more birds fly over the tree tops
No more place to hide in the woods
Gone is fairness in deliberation
Along with an opportunity to let it be

Hello to illusion and expansion
Goodbye to stability and conservation
The serpent of attachment devours the hills
With the treasures we took for granted

Today the smog still rolls in
The beach still covers in dust
A blade of grass pushes up from the ground
Maybe there's a regeneration
If she's resilient enough

Thank you for reading...

THE END

www.ingramcontent.com/pod-product-compliance
Lightning Source LLC
Chambersburg PA
CBHW021913040426
42447CB00007B/841